# PASS THE PARCEL

## Evacuee
## 1940-1945

## By Juliet Blick

Norden Books

Published in 2005 by
Norden Books
Hickory House  Penkridge Bank
RUGELEY     WS15 2UB
Tel: 01889 577799
e-mail: nordenbooks@yahoo.co.uk

ISBN  0-9550495-0-4

Printed by The Benhill Press Limited, Brook Square, Rugeley WS15 2DU
Tel: 01889 583240

# FOREWORD
### by the Author

The first time I put my thoughts and memories together about
my time as an evacuee, was in October 1997 when I was due to
give a talk at my local Over 50's Club. I was amazed how vivid
my memories were after all these years; I could even remember
all but one of my foster parents' names. Some of these have now
been changed, for obvious reasons. Although I found the whole
exercise quite traumatic, it was something I needed to do.

In January 1998 I enrolled on a Roots course with the Workers
Education Association (WEA) where one of the assignments was
an autobiography. I wrote about my time as an evacuee and it
was then made by them into a booklet titled 'Just Juliet', on
which this book is based. My reason for calling it 'Just Juliet' was
because as I wrote the story, I realised I was quite a naughty
child, like 'Just William' and 'Just Jane'. Now my memories will
never be lost. I would like my grandchildren and future
generations to read the story so that they will know what it was
like for me, and for many more children in Britain, during
wartime.

I like to think that they will never have to experience anything of
this sort for themselves.


*Juliet Blick*
*May 2005*

*My thanks go to*

My husband Clive, daughter Sally and son Kevin for their
help and encouragement in writing this book

My brother Bryan and sister Myriam for sharing their
memories with me

The WEA for giving me a kick-start with my writing.

After a troubled night, I wake up early in the morning with a start. I've had a dreadful nightmare. We children are no longer at home, but amongst strangers who talk like aliens from Mars. As I open my eyes and see the unfamiliar surroundings and Myriam sleeping beside me, I know I haven't been dreaming after all. It is reality. I am an EVACUEE!

The day war with Germany was declared (Sunday September 3rd 1939) lives with me forever. Our family was gathered together in our cosy bungalow in Westcliff-on-Sea, Essex, listening to the wireless. There was a look of shock and total disbelief on my parents' faces when it was announced. I didn't know what to think. Little did I realise then that in a very short time our lives would change forever, never again would we live together as a complete family.

My father, Julius was a German Jew, fluent in most European languages and he had started to teach us German. He travelled extensively in Europe on business, in fact he had just returned from Poland. He was in a hotel in the town of Cracow, the news was very disturbing and he was wondering whether to cut short his trip and return to England. Looking out of the hotel window, the sky was suddenly darkened by an enormous flock of crows. In Poland this was regarded as a bad omen so he returned to England immediately, just before the German invasion. Many of his relatives and close friends were not so lucky, they were now trapped in Europe.

I was the 'baby' of the family; my brother Bryan was born February 22nd (my mother's birthday too) 1929, sister Myriam born November 18th 1930, and I was born August 6th 1932. My father, Julius Norden, was a naturalised Englishman and, although he had lived in England for very many years, never lost his German accent. My mother Violet was working as a nurse when they married and was 22 years younger than my father. It was not a happy marriage.

We lived in Harpenden, near St Albans, until I was 5, and in those days it was quite rural, like living in the country, which we all loved. At that time we were living very comfortably. Car ownership at all in the 1930's was rare, and we had a large Minerva car, imported from Belgium. Bryan was attending Prep School and Myriam and I the Montessori. In 1937 Father's business in the hat trade in Luton failed, so it was imperative that in future we should lead a less expensive lifestyle. We moved to the Westcliff area of Southend-on-Sea Essex, as Father had discovered that the Southend state education system was one of the best in the country. Sadly, although he had the best of intentions, he could not have foreseen that the eventual outcome of this move would be tragic for all the family, except perhaps for Mother.

I was blissfully happy to be living by the sea, and remember it as one of the best times of my life. I don't think a day went by that we didn't go down to the beach, to play on the sand or swim in the sea. Even on school days during the summer, we children would meet Mother there at our dinner break and she would bring a picnic, which we eagerly devoured after our swim. Father, who was a great keep-fit fanatic, swam in the sea every day of the year, when he was around, and he would have us playing leapfrog, running races and generally rushing around. We rarely used towels to dry ourselves but were expected to race along the length of the beach until we were dry. I can see us now, all so brown and healthy, drinking in the ozone and hurtling about without a care in the world.

Imagine our horror then, with the outbreak of war, when we found our beloved beach covered in great coils of barbed wire. Mother was almost shot by a soldier who shouted "Halt! Who goes there?" when she tried to get on the beach. Thinking he was joking she ignored him and carried on, only stopping just in time! We were all issued with Gasmasks, Identity Cards and Ration Books, and Father had to build an Anderson shelter in the garden. This was basically a big pit with a corrugated steel roof and since our soil was heavy clay, our shelter was always damp inside. I don't remember ever using it except to play in.

We had to tape the house windows with strips of brown paper, in case they shattered if we were bombed. We also we put up heavy dark curtains for the Blackout, as no lights must be seen at night, in case of enemy planes. I was fascinated by the massive grey balloons floating in the sky, they were called Barrage Balloons and formed an anti-aircraft defence. I must say I was pleasantly surprised not to find men in the street fighting with guns, for this is what I imagined a war would be like. Mother returned to nursing locally and became a member of the Air Raid Precaution (ARP).

At the outbreak of war, London and other large cities were considered to be at risk of being bombed, so the children were evacuated to the countryside for safety, but when nothing much happened (it was called the Phoney War) many children returned home. However, by June 1940 France was occupied and a German invasion of England was feared, so children on the South Coast were evacuated as well. That of course included us. This it seems was only just in time as the Battle of Britain commenced soon after. Mother, still living in Westcliff and working as a nurse, was in the thick of the bombardment. By this time Father had taken off to the Midlands, as he was frightened of being captured by the Germans. They were never to live together again. I knew there was conflict between my parents but I always felt loved and cherished by both of them and being the youngest, I think I was rather spoilt.

*JULIET aged 10 MONTHS*

So at the age of seven, I was torn from the comfort and security of my family and home.

Evacuation Day was terrifying and to a seven year-old, all very confusing. I will never forget it. We each had a small rucksack, made by Mother. Mine contained one small book, a favourite toy, a small teddy bear, an apple and a packet of sandwiches, also a sponge bag, a change of underclothes and socks. We were all given a postcard to send home, as our parents had no idea of our destination. Name-tags were attached to our coats and of course we carried our gas masks; they went everywhere with us. We knew what to do as we had already had rehearsals through our school, which had closed as it was considered too dangerous for us to be far from home. Instead we had been having lessons from our teachers, in small groups, in the homes of different pupils. All signposts in Britain had by now been removed and church bells could only be rung as a sign of invasion.

We went to our school where everyone had gathered and were shepherded onto buses. Mothers and children were in tears, and the buses did a circular tour so that we could wave a last farewell, but there was no sign of our mother, she obviously hadn't realised this was to happen, and gone home. I felt very frightened and sad, why wasn't she there, where had she gone? The buses took us to Southend railway station, where there were hundreds more children and eventually we were herded on to the steam train, packed like sardines.

The journey seemed endless and Myriam suddenly said "You do realise that we will never see our parents again, don't you? We are going much too far away". "I don't believe you" I shouted and started to cry. This increased my feeling of terror and dread. At some of the larger stations, the Women's Voluntary Service (WVS) handed us drinks and sandwiches, which were very welcome as we had scoffed our own food soon after setting off. Also we were very thirsty, as we were not allowed to take drinks on the train, toilet facilities being very limited! Our train had to keep being shunted into sidings to let the scheduled trains through, making the journey take even longer. Eventually hours later, tired, grubby and dishevelled, we arrived at Derby station, where buses were waiting. Our big brother, Bryan, my hero and protector, tried so hard to stay with us, but he was dragged away, as boys and girls were to go to separate places. I am devastated and inconsolable. I want to go back home!

Bryan went to Hartshorne, near Swadlincote, Myriam and I to Overseal, near Burton-on-Trent. We were all taken to the village hall where we were to be 'chosen' by foster parents. As we were viewed, it felt as if we were in a cattle market. At the time I didn't realise that many of the families didn't welcome us, but if they had a spare bedroom, they had no option. Myriam and I were beginning to wonder if any-one wanted us, when eventually a childless couple named Butler chose us. There weren't many of us remaining by then.

That first night was dreadful, we couldn't understand what they were saying as they spoke so differently to us, it was like a foreign language. I was too tired and upset to eat anything, I just wanted a drink. In any case what on earth is that awful white stuff they have put in front of us, it looks like a piece of rubber. I was to encounter that many more times in the next 5 years. My stomach heaves now, as I see and smell that horrible thing they called food, it was of course, tripe! In our bedroom, the light bulb had been removed so that there was no need for Blackout curtains. As I lay crying in the bed I shared with Myriam, she is pointing to the sky. "See that cloud up there, well it isn't really a cloud, it's a Zeppelin coming to bomb us!" In abject terror, I clutch my tiny teddy so tightly and sob into his soft fur.

Some of the teachers from our school in Westcliff were evacuated with us, and the next morning all pupils and teachers meet in the village hall where we are asked the names of our foster parents. Myriam and I say in unison, "Mr and Mrs Bootler." "We have no-one of that name on our list, how do you spell it?" "I don't really know, like a boot I suppose," says my big sister. Why are they laughing at us? I can't see anything to even smile about, let alone laugh. The teacher, wiping tears from her eyes said, "You mean Mr and Mrs Batler". We all spoke like Londoners and will have to learn this new language!

Myriam and I went to different schools in the village, and one day we have a competition in our class, to see which of us can make the most words out of one very long word. The winner is to take a message down the road to the other school. I can't believe my luck; for years my father has been setting us this very task. That's easy, I can do it, I will show these village children I am good at something! Sure enough I win. I feel so proud walking down the village and into Myriam's classroom, but she looks a bit shocked. "Don't tell me I have got to put up with her," says her expression, "Now what is she up to?"

The toilet at the Butlers was downstairs, so we were given a chamber pot in the bedroom. We were told that if we did a wee in the toilet or the potty, we must not use toilet paper, "Don't you know there is a war on!" We couldn't cope with this so would take toilet paper upstairs, use the potty and throw the paper out of the window. We weren't to know that there was a water tank on a flat roof outside the bedroom window, and all the paper landed in there! Not surprisingly perhaps, we were called dirty little evacuees.

I think Mr Butler must have been a coal-miner because he used to get home from work, black from head to toe. We had never seen anything like this before and were fascinated. He would strip off in front of the fire and wash at the kitchen sink and as if by magic, there he was all pink and white again.

The Butlers were very religious people and we had to attend Chapel with them every Sunday. We all had to look very smart and dress in our best clothes. Perhaps my shoes were scuffed because I remember that Mrs Butler bought me a pair of black patent leather shoes to wear only for Chapel. I was so proud of them as I had never had posh shoes before, only practical ones. Myriam and I were not allowed to play outside on a Sunday.

Never having had children, the Butlers didn't seem to know how to treat us. They were very strict and appeared to resent us being there. Mother would send parcels unknown to us, but it seems that these were opened by the Butlers, before we even saw them. However, Myriam found that the contents were put in the box-room, and knew that they were intended for us. One day she took me up there and pointed to two toys, a cuddly rabbit and a rather hard white cat. She asked me which one I wanted, as we would get them eventually. "The cuddly rabbit" was my reply. "I knew you would choose that". says Myriam, who on the whole was very good to me. I remember that rabbit so well, it had a blue top and red trousers and a little smiling face, it went everywhere with me, when I eventually got it. When Mother came to visit us and saw how unhappy we were, she had us moved, but Mrs Butler made me leave my lovely shoes behind!

We then went to the home of Mr and Mrs Eyre, who lived on the outskirts of the village, overlooking fields. They had a daughter, Dorothy, probably about 18 and a son Frank aged 14. Dorothy went out to work, but I don't remember what she did and Frank had just left school. He was a butcher's delivery boy and had a bicycle with a large basket on the front, to carry the meat in. The bicycle was always tipping over (I suppose it easily overbalanced) and all the meat would fall out. Frank would come home crying, for help to sort out the dirty meat! However he took great delight in teasing me, but I couldn't cope with that and would frequently 'run away from home' down the lane. Dorothy or her parents always came rushing after me.

Mr and Mrs Eyre were so very kind and, being an older couple, almost like grandparents to us. Myriam and I were really happy there. I remember one day, after doing some sewing, I left a needle in the chair and poor Mr Eyre got it stuck in his bottom. He had to suffer the indignity of having it removed by his wife, but they weren't even cross with me. On the way home from school, I used to run through great mounds of lime, piled up in the fields. Imagine what I would have looked like, white from head to toe. What a wretched child I must have been, but I never remember being told off.

We used to sit at night in Dorothy's bedroom, watching the air raids over Derby when we were supposed to be sheltering under the table. I found it quite exciting, but I was rather apprehensive too. We could see the searchlights with aeroplanes caught in the beams, hear the anti-aircraft guns, the sound of bombs exploding and, most frightening of all, the drone of German planes. That is something I cannot forget. Occasionally, Mrs Eyre took us on the bus to do some shopping in Burton-on-Trent, which was and still is, famous for it's breweries. The delicious smell of malt is a lasting memory.

My 8th birthday arrived on August 6th 1940 and for the first time I was going to have to celebrate a birthday away from home. We had always been made to feel so special, how would I cope? Mother couldn't be there as the Battle of Britain was imminent. However, Father came and I remember we sat in a field in brilliant sunshine just talking. Myriam was there of course and oh, what joy, Bryan came over from Hartshorne on his bike. We were almost a family again and I still have those 8th birthday cards from Father, Bryan and Myriam, they survived the war. It was then that Father made us promise never to tell anyone that he was German and especially a German Jew; we must tell people that he was a Dutchman. Foolishly, sometime later, I was to break that promise.

*BRYAN, JULIET AND MYRIAM*
*OUTSIDE THE HOUSE AT HARPENDEN*

Bryan cycled over to see Myriam and me whenever he could and told us that in his village the local boys used to lie in wait for the evacuees, chasing them with sticks and calling them names, like 'horrid little vaccies'. It was made worse for Bryan, after our father had been to visit him. This was due to his funny foreign accent, and because he had a habit of sitting in the middle of a field during the day on his own, writing, while waiting for Bryan to come out of school. The boys even thought Father could be a German spy.

Before we left Westcliff our parents had applied to send us on the

Overseas Evacuation Scheme and we were selected to go to
Canada. We even got as far as having a medical in Derby. Bryan
remembers that he was waiting at the bus stop in Hartshorne
early one morning, to go for his medical, when he saw an
enormous aeroplane fly over, very slowly, only about 60 feet off
the ground. When it was over the next village, Melbourne, he
saw 4 shapes like parachutes, fall from it. When the bus arrived
at Melbourne, he was shocked to see that the village had been
bombed and a pub, full of soldiers, had received a direct hit.
It was a German aeroplane, a Dornier, and it was just off loading
it's bombs before returning home.

In September 1940 a ship, the City Of Benares, on route to Canada
with 300 people on board, including evacuees, was torpedoed. 260
perished including 84 children and only 7 children survived. The
sad thing was that many of those children had previously been on
another ship, the Volendam, which had been torpedoed on the
30th August. They had all survived that, and waited for the next
ship, only to perish. Consequently the official Overseas
Evacuation Scheme was stopped, but I often think how different
our lives would have been had we gone to Canada.

While still in Westcliff Bryan had taken the scholarship exam and
good for him, had passed. The whole of the Southend High
School was evacuated to Mansfield, a mining town in
Nottinghamshire, and Father decided that Bryan must go of
course. He also felt it was vital that we three children stay
together, so decided that we should all go to Mansfield.

Our happiness with life in the countryside and with the
delightful Eyre family came to an abrupt end.

This was the beginning of a nightmare, and after all these years I
have only to hear the name MANSFIELD and my stomach does a
double somersault.

Mansfield was far removed from the rural life in Overseal. Myriam and I went to the homes of two brothers named Greaves, who lived next door to each other. From what Myriam has told me, it seems the brothers' wives didn't get on and went for long periods without speaking to each other. In my billet was a daughter Elsie, about my age, and there was an older boy Basil, away serving in the Navy. At the other house were a small girl Pat, aged about 5 or 6, and a boy Malcolm, probably about 9. Myriam had to share a bed with Pat, who most nights wet the bed and consequently wet Myriam too!

Elsie told me, when we were going to school the next day, to say that I had been in the 'A' stream, then I would be in the same class as her. I dutifully did this, even though I had never heard of 'A' and 'B' streams, but I was told that for the time being, I must go into the 'B' class until there was a place for me in the 'A' class. My teacher was Mr Crossland, he was wonderfully kind and gentle, he was so good to me and I adored him. I see him now, standing there quite tall, a little stooped, grey hair and glasses, wearing a well-worn tweed jacket. He was quietly spoken, no need for him to shout to get our attention or keep us in order. At Christmas he gave me a lovely card and a pretty blue patterned hanky, how I treasured them. I felt I was getting on quite well with my schooling.

One dreadful day, I was told that a place was now available in the 'A' class. How I wished that I hadn't lied that very first day. I had to sit next to this boy at a double desk. I feel frightened and I am sad to leave my lovely Mr Crossland. Now we have a lady teacher and she is shouting all the time. They are doing maths and something called Problems, what does that mean? I don't know what they are talking about. I have never done Problems. I daren't tell anyone, so I try to copy my desk-mate's work. "Miss she is cheating" he shouts. I get a rap on the knuckles with a ruler. I never did catch up in Maths and have struggled with that subject all my life.

However, I did consider I was quite good at spelling at that school. One day we had a spelling test and one of the words was August. Being a rather boastful child I shouted, "I know that one because it is my birthday month." You have guessed it, I got it wrong, I cringe at the memory.

Mid morning lunch snacks were placed on the table in the classroom to avoid the temptation of eating them during lessons, but I of course never had any to take. One day all that was left on this table was a Crunchy Bar and my desk-mate says "You can have that chocolate bar, I don't want it after all." I can't believe he is being so kind to me and waste no time biting into it. Halfway through it, in walks this girl. "Where is my Crunchy Bar?" I can't hide. "Miss she has stolen my lunch." More trouble! I am now branded a thief as well as a cheat and no-one believes me when I try to explain. Is there no end to my misery? It took me many years before I could face a Crunchy Bar again.

I have had enough of these kids! I have to do *something* to make them like me, feel sorry for me or perhaps be my friends. It's time to go home from school and I know what I will do. "Anyway, my father is a German Jew," I shout, at the top of my voice. Why are they looking so shocked and angry? "Let's get her!" Fortunately I could run very fast in those days, hadn't I had plenty of training on the beach at Westcliff? I am sure if they had caught up with me before I got home, they would have lynched me. I had to say, the next day, that I was only joking. I had certainly learnt my lesson and now understood what my father had meant.

One day I saw something crawling on my desk-mate's shoulders. The following day my foster mother noticed crawly things in my hair. I had nits! She was so angry with me, she made me use my own pocket money, go to the chemist and buy the stuff to treat it. I was very unpopular or should I say more so than usual.

I have one particularly unpleasant memory of my time living at Elsie's house. They had a small dog and at night it would soil the living room floor. Elsie and I were always first up in the mornings, and as the light switch to the room was across the other side, we would edge round keeping close to the wall, in our bare feet, hoping we would reach the switch without treading in something unpleasant. We weren't always successful!

It wasn't a happy household and I think my being there, strained things even further. Elsie and I couldn't get on so it was decided that I should move in next door with Myriam. It was almost Christmas and there was a new Panda storybook on the table. We asked who it was for and Aunty said it was for a little girl she knew. So we asked if we could read it and one by one we did so. Christmas Eve came, Myriam and I were sharing a bed, and I whispered to her when I saw some one creeping about. The next morning everyone had a stocking but me, as I had been talking and naughty girls don't get stockings from Father Christmas. I never did get that stocking but I did get one present, the Panda book that we had all read. I was 8 years old at the time.

One night in bed, Myriam and I were trying to get warm. I said to Myriam, "You give me some more blanket and I will give you some eiderdown." The door burst open, "I heard what you said", yelled Aunty, "you wrap yourself in the blanket and I will wrap myself in the eiderdown." She was so angry with us, she had obviously been listening outside the door and thought we were going to destroy the bedding.

While we were living there, our parents were fighting a case in the Courts, for the custody of we three children. Mrs Greaves or Aunty as we called her, was told by our mother that under no circumstances was she to allow Father to see us. One evening, when we children were in bed, I heard shouting and recognised Father's voice. Then the door slammed and I heard him going down the road, sobbing loudly and saying "My chillern, my chillern" in his German way. Those anguished cries will haunt me forever.

*HAPPIER DAYS WITH MOTHER*

At around this time, Father 'kidnapped' Bryan and took him to live with him somewhere in Nottinghamshire. However Aunty and Mother managed to find him, removed him and hid him away. It was then decided that for the time being, Myriam and I should also be removed from our billet, to a place of safety.

Myriam and I were taken to the Vicarage at Edwinstowe, which is in Sherwood Forest. What bliss, we were back in the countryside again.

We loved the area and found it great fun to explore the forest and go inside Robin Hood's enormous oak tree, we went there often. The Vicar Mr Haslar, and his wife, were extremely kind people, and they had a daughter Mary, a school teacher. They were all so good to us and we were so very happy there. We attended the village school and although we found they were a year behind us educationally, we felt very welcome and revelled in the village life.

The Vicarage was an enormous rambling place. I can picture us now, rushing up the main staircase, along the lengthy corridor and down the maid's staircase, playing hide and seek or sliding down the beautifully polished banister. The Haslars must have wondered what they had taken on and been quite apprehensive, as they had a house full of treasures. But they never seemed to reprimand us or get annoyed and they were so patient with us. I was in a bit of trouble once, however when I told the children at school that the Haslars only had half a maid. The poor girl had a withered arm! I do remember Mrs Haslar inspecting Myriam and me for fleas, she had found a spot of blood on my pyjama top but fortunately it was a false alarm.

However our happy times at the Vicarage were not to last. After a few months, Mother was granted custody of all three children and it was decided that we should return to the dreaded MANSFIELD.

Myriam and I went to a couple called Bentley who had a small daughter aged about three. It was Myriam's task every evening to stay with this girl until she was asleep. Every time she tried to creep out of the room, the small girl would wake up and cry, it took Myriam ages to settle her. I especially remember at this house, the horrible heated-up dinners. They must have been put in the oven on a plate, from mid-day until we got home at tea time. I can still smell and taste those horrible dinners, especially the dried-up cabbage.

One Saturday, Mrs Bentley, the small girl and Myriam went shopping and I stayed behind with Mr Bentley. Mrs Bentley asked me to prepare the potatoes while they were out, ready for lunch. They were new potatoes and not knowing any better, I started to peel them. A very angry Mr Bentley comes into the kitchen. "What do you think you are doing, surely you know better than that?" "Oh I know what I am supposed to do now, scrape them." "Just leave them alone, don't touch them anymore." "Please let me do them!" It was no good. I was in terrible trouble when Mrs Bentley arrived home and found the potatoes weren't ready.

Here was another family who kept our parcels sent to us by Mother. It was Myriam's birthday and she watched the postman call at the house with cards and a parcel. Her birthday came and went and she had nothing. When Mother came to visit us some time later and once more saw how unhappy we were, she went to the Billeting Officer and had us moved.

Our next home was with a young widow, Mrs Kirkwood, a hairdresser who made it very plain from the start that she did not want us. She had a boyfriend who spent a lot of time there and Myriam and I would have to stay outside, whatever the weather, while she entertained him. I remember once going downstairs late at night, for a glass of water and seeing them canoodling; I was in real trouble. She gave him our food rations and we were always hungry, so our mother complained to the authorities about her behaviour. Soon after, we came back from a weekend away, to find all our belongings thrown outside in the rain. We were not sorry to be leaving.

By now things were getting very difficult, as there were so many evacuees in the area and billets were in very short supply. Mrs Greaves said she would take Myriam back, but no way did she want *me*! So Myriam returned to the Greaves and stayed with them for the remainder of the war.

She wasn't particularly happy there and has told me about some of the unpleasant things that happened. Due to the fact that her schooling finished late, she would be given bread and jam for tea, when the rest of the family had had pilchards on toast etc. Also Aunty took great delight in 'reporting' that she had overheard people in queues talking about our parents being separated (frowned on in those days) and our father being a German Jew. Obviously this was just to taunt Myriam and make her feel unwanted, as it could not possibly have been true.

OCTOBER 1938

My next home was in a very deprived area of Mansfield. This is the only one of my 10 billets where I don't remember the lady's name. However I do remember she lived on her own, was very fat and was quite kind to me. I played in the street with other children where there was a fish and chip shop with this horrible stale greasy smell coming from it. Around this time, I began to get dreadful pains in my legs. I was told that they were growing pains (I've since learned there is no such thing) and had to wear thick black stockings. Somehow my mother discovered that at some stage, my foster mother had had Tuberculosis and perhaps still had it. Since there was only one bedroom and I had to share the bed with her it was imperative that I be moved immediately.

My 9th billet was with a dear little elderly lady, called Mrs Tallon. She really was a sweetie, so kind and compassionate, she made me very welcome and I really loved her. I slept in an enormous, sparsely furnished bedroom at the front of the house, right on the roadside and when the buses went by at night, the whole room would light up. In this bedroom there was a huge walk-in cupboard and I always imagined that someone could be hiding in there; I found that a bit frightening.

It was a terraced house and next door lived Mrs Tallon's son and family. They had a daughter Muriel, about my age, and she and I became great playmates. I still have a lovely big illustrated book that she gave me for Christmas 1943, 'Rumanian Fairy Tales'. At the back of the book are some drawings, to illustrate other books in the series. I couldn't resist colouring two of them in with crayons, and I still feel guilty when I look at them. Muriel was very annoyed with me and told me one should never do anything to deface a book, even though I did colour the pictures very carefully. To this day I won't even put a message inside a book that I am giving as a present. Amazingly, I also still have a book in the same series, given to us three children by our father in December 1938, titled 'Stories from the Bible'. He has written the date and messages inside in Hebrew and English and I am so glad that he did.

Next to Mrs Tallon's son lived her daughter and that was the end of the terrace, with the side window facing onto another street. In this street, very near to the house, was a concrete air raid shelter and I used to throw a ball against it. One day, my ball landed on top of the flat roof and stayed there. As I only had the one ball, I decided to throw a stone onto the roof to try to dislodge the ball, the stone flew right over the shelter and straight through the daughter's window. Looking furtively around, hoping I hadn't been seen, I took off as fast as my legs would carry me, I didn't go back for a very long time. When I did, Muriel told me some horrible person had broken Aunty's window, by throwing a stone through it. I dare not admit that I was that horrible person, but I wonder even now, if it is too late to confess!

This street rose very steeply and I used to pretend that if I kept going, I would be able to see the sea over the brow of the hill. Myriam told me she used to have a recurring dream that she had found her way back to our cosy bungalow in Westcliff. We were all in the kitchen, the smell of baking filled the room, Mother was quietly ironing and everything was back to normal. It was our way of keeping our memories alive and our hope for the future.

Muriel's Aunty was an usherette at the local cinema. This was a great boon to us as it meant that when we went to the Twopenny Rush every Saturday we were allowed to sit in the sixpenny seats for twopence, what luxury. It was at Mrs Tallon's that I first had supper, my last meal had always been tea. "What is this? fruit cake and cheese, I've never eaten them together before, I don't know if I fancy that." "Go on, try it" "Oh, it's lovely." Mrs Tallon (I don't ever remember calling her Aunty, as we did most foster mothers) used to do a lot of baking. Muriel and I would frequently have doll's tea parties, with real cakes and pastries cut into tiny portions, our favourite being Bakewell Tart. After the dolls had eaten their fill, we would polish off the remains!

It was during one of these tea parties that Muriel suddenly said, "Nan, what is going to happen to Juliet when you move into your Old People's bungalow?" Shocked silence all round and I begin to cry. Apparently, well before I arrived on the scene, dear little Mrs. Tallon had put in for this special one-bedroom bungalow and hadn't known how to tell me that it was now available. I am distraught, why is it that every time I think I have found real happiness it falls apart?

By now there were no billets left but Bryan, my hero comes to the rescue. He has been living in various billets in Mansfield and used to keep running away on his bicycle and going to see Mother, who by now was nursing in the Midlands. For the last year or so, he has been with a family named Sage, Valerie and Gordon, and their son Barry. They have a little white dog, called Barney, a highly-strung pedigree Sealyham that is always having fits. I have been to visit Bryan there quite often, so know the family well and Bryan very kindly offers to move to a hostel for 'Bad Boys', so that I can go and live at the Sages.

Valerie, or Aunty, as I called her, was very kind and good to me, but quite strict, and not very motherly. She always seemed to have some ailment, and would go around holding her head or stomach, and most of the time looking quite ill. It seemed to me then, that she wouldn't last long; however she lived to the good old age of 92. Gordon, or Uncle, worked for the Co-op as a baker's roundsman, using a horse-drawn cart. He was a very jolly man, fairly plump with a happy smiling face and would come home, late afternoon, always in a very jovial mood. It is only in recent years that I learned from Valerie, that he was actually coming home tipsy!

*MYRIAM AND JULIET IN THE BROWNIES*

Barry was Bryan's age, about 3 years older than me, he was
quite a strange boy and I felt he preferred Bryan's company to
mine. However, we got on quite well until one very memorable
day. Barry and I were supposed to be doing piano practice in
the front room (we were having piano lessons) when we
decided to have some fun. Barry carried me around on his
shoulders, making monkey noises and it was all quite innocent.
Suddenly the door burst open, and Aunty hurtled into the room,

in a dreadful rage. "What do you two think you are doing?" I was thrown on the floor and Barry looking thoroughly ashamed, tried to get out of the room. His way was blocked by Aunty, who said "Don't you ever let me find you two alone together again." It was only in recent years that it has occurred to me why Aunty was so angry. She must have been terrified that we might get up to hanky-panky. Certainly, nothing was further from *my* mind! The piano lessons came to an abrupt end soon after anyway, because the piano teacher became pregnant. I never took up piano playing again.

From then on, Barry was vile to me. Most of the time he ignored me; I was told not to speak unless I was spoken to and he was always getting me into trouble with Aunty. We had to cook our own breakfast and were only supposed to fry bread on one side, due to the rationing. I would pretend that the fish slice had slipped as I was getting the bread out of the frying pan so I could get fat on both sides. Barry watched me like a hawk and would then tell Aunty what I'd done. He would tell her if I went upstairs in the day, as we were only supposed to go down and up once a day in case we wore out the stair carpet (this was the routine in most of our billets). Barry never lost an opportunity to get at me.

Amongst the photographs in my bedroom was one I really treasured, of my mother in her nurse's uniform. It is bed time and I am looking longingly at my mother's beautiful face, wondering if we will ever be together again, will this war never end? What has happened to her face? Someone has made holes through her lovely hazel eyes, her nostrils, and her mouth. Who could do such a thing? Only one person, Barry! I still have that photo. The first time he really spoke to me again was 50 years later when he telephoned to tell me his mother had died. He never married but stayed at the family home, caring for his mother.

Aunty was a very good dressmaker, and I loved watching her at work, especially when she was making wedding and bridesmaid dresses. I can see that room now, filled to capacity with frothy material and lace, goodness knows where she got it all from. I have to keep well back, I am only allowed to stand at the door. One very exciting day, I am invited into the room. I am to have two new dresses, made by Aunty and I have to be measured. Oh, I can't believe it! "Will you stand still, how can I possibly measure you if you keep dancing up and down?" My dresses won't be pastel shades and frilly of course, but darker and practical, never mind, I know I'll just love them. One will be blue with white spots, the other red with white spots. How impatient I am to see them finished and how proud I am when I finally wear the blue one first; that was always my favourite.

Aunty used to cut my hair and always made me have it really short. I didn't think much of that, and one of the first things I did at the end of the war was to grow my hair long. We lived further out of town than Myriam, and one day a friend of hers invited us both to a birthday party. I had to get on the bus higher up the road and when Myriam got on the bus and saw me, she was almost in shock! My hair was shorter than usual and what a sight I looked, but worse was to come. It was a wet day and Aunty had made me wear wellingtons! "I ask you", said a furious Myriam, "fancy coming to a party in wellingtons, I feel so ashamed of you, going to my friend's house looking like a tramp." That night Aunty was helping me get undressed. "I hope you haven't been cocking your legs about, you have holes in your knickers!" I didn't dare tell her (until a few years ago) that I had been doing just that. It was a good party (in spite of the wellingtons, which I had removed!) and we had all got very excited. We ended up doing somersaults over the back of the settee. It is to be hoped that Myriam didn't spot the holes in my knickers, but I feel I would have heard about it if she had!

I remember coming home from school and wanting to chat about my day. Aunty said "For goodness sake, can't you talk about anything else, I'm sick of hearing about school". I was very hurt, what else have I got to talk about and who else have I got to talk to? After that, I used to get home, deliberately start talking about school, and then say "Oh I forgot, I'm not supposed to talk about that". What an unpleasant child I was, but I was just trying to get my own back.

The Sages and I all moved house, just a short distance away and in the garden was a greenhouse, full of ripe tomatoes. We had tomatoes at every meal, day after day, I've never eaten so many in my life. My poor stomach objected and one night I had a severe bilious attack and was sick all over the bed. Not wanting to disturb anybody, I just got in the other end of the bed. The next morning there was this horrible dried up mess, and Aunty was not at all pleased. She said that she would rather have dealt with it at the time, "What was I thinking of?"

I found some new playmates, when we moved. I remember talking to these girls, in the road, about playing in the quad (quadrangle) at school. They started to giggle and said "You had better ask your foster mother to tell you all about babies". Said I, boasting as usual, "I know all about babies, my mother is a midwife!" In actual fact, I knew very little, and what I did know had gleaned from Myriam. Aunty frequently would say "I expect your mother has told you all about growing up." "Oh yes," I would reply. However, I could never bring myself to talk to Mother about such things, but found it easier to talk to Myriam, who got all the information from Mother and passed it on to me! I remember finding some 'balloons' on the ground in a park and was about to blow one up when Myriam stopped me and told me what they really were, I was still a bit puzzled!

Aunty taught me quite a lot of things in my time with her. Since she was always suffering from something or other and Uncle was seldom there, Barry and I had to do quite a lot of the household chores. One thing I especially remember was her showing me how to light a fire, with newspaper and sticks. Once they had started burning, I tended to put the coal on too quickly. "You must let it breath," said Aunty, "Just dot the coal around until it has taken hold". I was always a good 'fire-lighter' after that.

The highlight of my time with the Sages was the outings we had to their relatives in the country. We went on quite a long bus journey and then had to walk down the lane before arriving at their cottage. Everything was always warm and cosy in there, and the appetising smell of the dinner cooking would greet us as we walked through the door. I always saved some of my meagre sweet ration to spend at the village shop. To get there I had to go across a field and there it was, snuggling down a dip, all on it's own. I think it was just a cottage with the front room as a shop. How I would gaze through the window at the well stocked display, such a variety, and inside the shop even more. How is it that I see sweets here that I never see anywhere else? I can't make up mind, it takes me forever, but I always end up with the same, my very favourite, toffee nut crunch.

Early in 1944 my life changed dramatically. London was being bombarded with Doodlebugs (flying bombs) and V2 rockets, launched from France and Holland, and there was a desperate need to evacuate any remaining children from the London area. Aunty decided she could squeeze in one small boy who could share a room with Barry, so my nose was really put out of joint. I was no longer the only evacuee but had to share with this horrible, scruffy little cockney. I don't like him, I am really jealous, why did he have to come and spoil things for me? His nose is always running and he wipes it on his sleeve but the very worst thing is that he uses *my* flannel and leaves it in the wash basin, swimming in slimy black water. I won't stand for *that*. Aunty sits me down and explains to me that I must try very hard to be kind and sympathetic because this poor boy needs her help just as much as I do, perhaps more so. I do understand and I *will* try harder, but I still don't like him and she has to stop him using my flannel! Fortunately, he didn't stay too long, in fact very few evacuees stayed away for the duration of the war, as we three did. Many returned home as soon as things eased off in their area. In June 1944 the Allied troops landed in France, so the danger from the air abated and most evacuees, from all over Britain began to return home, but not us of course. Where could we go?

*VIOLET DURING THE WAR*

Both Myriam and I took the scholarship exam for the Southend High School, which was at the time evacuated to the Queen Elizabeth Grammar School for Girls in Mansfield. I now realise that this was because Father wanted to make sure that we still had the benefit of the Southend education, which had been his dream, and it had been expected that we would eventually all return to Westcliff. We both had to take the exam on our own, a year apart, in the Headmaster's room, and Myriam remembers that she was told not to leave the room under any circumstances. She was desperate to do a wee, couldn't wait any longer, and wet her pants. On his return, the Headmaster found it quite amusing to see this puddle on the floor!

When I took the exam, there was an air raid warning in the middle of it, and we all had to troop down to the shelter, very off putting. The dreadful undulating wail of the siren always filled me with dread and what a relief it would be to hear the even tone of the all clear. When I had finished the exam, I remember the Headmaster and my teacher looking at my papers and shaking their heads. Oh well, that's me done for, I thought. However, I did pass, as Myriam had done the previous year, what a relief.

When at Westcliff, Father had promised each of us a pony if we passed the scholarship. With the war, this became an impossible dream, (I wonder now if he ever really meant it) so instead he had promised us £5, a lot of money in those days. Myriam and Bryan didn't tell me whether or not they had been given their reward, but the first time I saw Father, after hearing I had passed, before even greeting him, I said "You owe me five pounds!" He was very angry as we hadn't seen each other for quite a long time and it wasn't the sort of greeting he was expecting. I never did get my fiver!

When Myriam started at the Grammar School, Southend pupils had to share school time with the Mansfield pupils. She went from 1-30 to 5-30 Monday to Friday and 9-00 to 1-30 on Saturday. She didn't have her own desk, (we always used to in those days) and had to carry her books everywhere with her. She had a lot of extra homework to compensate for the short hours at school. However, by the time I went, most of the Southend pupils had returned home, so my school hours were normal.

I quite enjoyed my time there, but one lesson I really hated was Art; I was hopeless and could barely draw a straight line and still can't! One day, to amuse the rest of the pupils, I painted my face instead of painting a picture. Nowadays it's quite fashionable but it wasn't then. "Right, straight to the Headmistress you go," said a very angry Art Teacher. Now I've done it, I've gone too far this time. I have to stand outside the Headmistress's room for what seems an eternity but eventually I am called in. Will she laugh at my painted face? Far from it, she is not amused and I get a very long lecture, ending with "We don't really want you at this school, we didn't have to take you let me tell you, but only did so because your sister is here and we felt sorry for you. Any more trouble and you are out, understand? Go back to your class, after washing your face, and apologise to your teacher." After that lot I feel very alone and sorry for myself. I get no support from Myriam, when she hears about it. She is a star pupil, very well behaved, good at all subjects particularly Art, she is ashamed of me!

During our time as evacuees, we did have some good holidays. We spent some happy times with our grandparents in Surrey, and I never wanted to leave them to return to my billet. We also stayed with our Aunty Joyce in Coventry, travelling there by steam train. We were very shocked to see all the bomb damage, the lovely Cathedral was just a shell, and there were houses with rooms open to the elements. The town centre was all but destroyed and Woolworth's continued to trade in the cellar. Rosebay Willowherb, (also known as Fireweed), was sprouting everywhere, amongst the debris on the bomb sites. Whenever I see it now, it reminds me of the war years. We had to sleep on a mattress on the floor, as Aunty Joyce didn't have a spare bedroom. She had to keep the mattress under the stairs and it was always damp, even though she tried to air it in front of the electric fire.

*BRIDLINGTON 1942 WITH ALLAN MY FIRST LOVE*

We also went to stay with our relatives in Norfolk, on their farm. Our mother asked a friend with a car to take us there. The farm was a whole new experience and one that we children revelled in. Aunt Edie, Uncle Jack and their three sons and families made us very welcome. One son, Jack and family lived in a cottage on the farm and had three children. Another son, Tom, lived in a cottage a short distance away, with his wife Margaret and he also worked on the farm. The third son, Bill and his family lived in the next village and he helped on the farm very occasionally. There was a fourth son, Dick, but he was away in the Air Force, and I never did meet him. I loved the way they talked, "Now, goo you abed" little Aunt Edie would say at bedtime.

With the dew still on the grass, we would get up early, to go mushrooming and bring them to Aunt Edie, who cooked them for our breakfast. We would race around the fields and see who could fill their basket first, heedless of our soaking wet feet; we should have worn our wellingtons. The smell of the freshly picked mushrooms cooking and the taste as we ate them is something I can only dream about now. I learned to drive the tractor and to hand milk the cows. One day when we were all helping with the harvest, I had the prestigious job of driving the tractor very slowly whilst everyone else picked up the sheaves and loaded them onto the trailer. Just as the trailer was fully laden, I drove down a dip, the trailer tipped sideways and the whole load fell to the ground. It was a while before I was allowed on the tractor again!

Probably the most thrilling thing for me was riding home from the fields, at the end of the day, on the back of one of the massive, gentle Shire horses. I can see for miles around from up here. I feel so proud and so very special, I can pretend I am a queen. If I dare take one hand off the mane for a moment, I can wave to my subjects! One thing I did find quite amusing; some way from the farm house was a shed and inside was a double chemical toilet, I had never seen such a thing. I had visions of a couple of ladies sitting side by side chatting to each other, perhaps knitting even, as they did their duty!

Mother, who was by now doing midwifery, moved around the country working at different locations. Whenever possible, she would have us to stay in the area for an occasional break. Sometimes all three of us went together, another time it could be Myriam and me and sometimes we went separately. In that case we took it in turns. I tried so hard not to get too excited when it was my turn to go because it seemed to me that if I did, something always went wrong. The desperation I felt if my trip had to be cancelled was unbelievable.

One of the happiest holiday times was spent at Bridlington, we were actually allowed on the beach! Oh what magic, it is like being at Westcliff again. We stay with a really nice family named Pashby, and there is a boy called Allan, quite a bit smaller and younger than me. I fall madly in love with him and I will definitely marry him when I grow up! It is my 10th Birthday and Bryan, Myriam and Allan are all sitting around the table, making birthday cards for me. I try not to peep, I can't wait for them to finish. At last they are ready, Allan has drawn an elephant, Bryan a Dutchman in the bulb fields, and Myriam a most artistic one with a fancy duck posting a card into a red letter box and it says 'To my dear sister' on the duck's envelope. Each card has a rhyme inside, they mean so much to me and I will treasure them forever. In fact I do still have those cards.

Another place we stayed at was in a village called Gate Burton, near Gainsborough, in Lincolnshire. Mother was nursing at Gate Burton Hall, a stately home. Most of these places were taken over during the war to be used as schools, hospitals, for evacuees (lucky things) or for the army etc. We were allowed to go to the Hall with our mother and felt overawed by the splendour of the place and the size of the rooms. The grounds were fantastic and we would run around exploring to our heart's content. Those were carefree days.

Great excitement on one very special day I will never forget. There is to be a dance at the Hall, and I am invited! I am about to attend my first real grown up dance, but what shall I wear? It will have to be my pretty blue and white spotted dress that Aunty made me and I will wear a matching blue hairband made from ribbon, in my hair. There is a girl there, about my age, called Daphne and we dance with each other all evening. I have never been taught to dance but she shows me how to waltz, "One two three, one two three." The Quickstep follows, then the Foxtrot and an Old Time Waltz, "Just quicken your steps it's easy". I get more and more excited as the night wears on and then it was the Tango. "You can't do that," says Daphne, "It's much too difficult." "I can do anything, I know I can do it," I boasted. Daphne was right of course, I tripped over her feet trying to follow her and, domino-like, caused several of the grown-ups to fall flat on the crowded floor, along with Daphne and me!

Birthdays were a difficult time, when we were evacuated. We had a small amount of pocket money, sent to us by our mother, but most of that went on our sweet ration. It is Myriam's birthday tomorrow and I am penniless, what shall I do? I know, I will give her all my special treasures. I find a little box and line it with cotton wool. In goes my favourite marble, a large blue and green one, a pretty brooch, a tiny gold coloured baby, a plum pudding doll (tiny white china doll, used instead of silver threepenny bits during the war) and last of all, my dainty gold chain link bracelet. Father had given both of us one of these bracelets and Myriam has lost hers. I feel very pleased with myself, and also very self-righteous. Myriam is quite overwhelmed with all these gifts but also very surprised. The next day I am devastated, what was I thinking of, what have I done, how could I be so stupid? As soon as I see Myriam, I shout "Please can I have my treasures back?" "I was waiting for that," says Myriam "I knew this would happen, you can have everything back except the bracelet." I plead with her, I try crying but it's no good, she won't change her mind. I suppose I am lucky to get anything back.

*MYRIAM AND JULIET AT GATE BURTON HALL*


After all these years, I still long for that bracelet. However I do still today have my 'gold' baby and my plum pudding doll. I also have a little china figure of a nurse in uniform that Myriam and I bought between us. It was to give to our mother, when she passed her midwifery exams, but sad to say she never did pass. I think she had too stressful a time with court cases, trying to get maintenance for us etc., as well as working and trying to keep an eye on us.

The end of the war in Europe came at last! VE Day May 8th 1945. The cease-fire in Japan (VJ Day) didn't take place for another three months. The war had lasted so long, almost six years and at times we all despaired but never gave up hope. Now is the time for jubilation, down come the Blackout curtains and strips of brown paper criss-crossing the windows. Up go the banners and balloons, the flags and the bunting. Then the street parties begin.

What a time we have, where has all this food come from? Tables the length of the street, laden with food I haven't seen since before the war. People must have been hoarding it and keeping it for just this occasion. After eating we dance the night away and I fall into bed thinking I can go home tomorrow.

I wake up in the morning and realise I haven't got a home to go to.

Father has bought a house in Beeston, near Nottingham, hoping that one day we will all go to live there and be a family again, but Mother has other ideas. She now has full custody of we three children and having obtained a legal separation, has no intention of ever going back to our father. The war has enabled her to get out of a very unhappy marriage and that is how it will remain. She had no home of course as she was expected to live in, at her place of work. So meantime we have no choice but to stay at our billets, with the agreement of our foster parents.

After three long months, we have a home! Our mother has a very good friend, we call him Uncle Bill, and he is willing to take us all on. He lives in a cottage in a Lincolnshire village called Sturton-by-Stow, and we have already met him and in fact been to stay with him. So we go back to the country life and how! There is no running water, just a pump in the garden, a chemical toilet, no electricity, only oil lamps and candles, and all cooking is done on the coal fire range. We also have to take our bath in front of the fire in a tub! Apart from the toilet, I find it quite fun and certainly quite a challenge. We are back with our mother again, what bliss, I have to pinch myself to make sure it isn't a dream! Bryan by now had finished his schooling. Myriam and I were transferred to Lincoln High School for Girls, where we found we were behind in Latin. We had to spend the summer holidays catching up.

I kept in touch with the Reverend Haslar and his wife until they died and for a while afterwards with their daughter Mary. I also kept in touch with Valerie Sage by phone calls and correspondence. We never did meet up again, although we almost did on one or two occasions. I got the feeling that she didn't really want to and in a way it was nice for me to remember her as she was. She died some years ago, aged 92, and her son Barry has since been to see us and phones now and again. He just wanted to talk about his mother and I felt no bitterness towards him.

I have to say that it was only a few years ago that I really stopped to think just what a dramatic effect evacuation had on so many people, not just us children. It must have been terrible for our parents, I honestly don't think I would have been able to let my children go, and thank goodness I have never had to make that decision. Our foster parents must have found it an unbelievable disruption to their lives, especially the ones who really didn't want us. I can't imagine anything worse than having strange children foisted on one for an indefinite period and I love children! Whatever must it have been like to be a Billeting Officer? So it goes on. My brother in law told me a funny story, which illustrates how desperate some people were to avoid having evacuees. He was evacuated from Surrey to relatives in Bradford and the Billeting Officer was due to call at every house to check on the number of spare bedrooms. The next door neighbours didn't want any evacuees, so 'borrowed' young Peter for the night. What with the blackout and being in a strange house, he couldn't find the toilet so did a wee on the landing floor. Later he heard the sound of scrubbing, they got their just deserts!

I did actually apologise to Valerie Sage, in recent years, for all the trouble I had been and thanked her for all that she had done for me, and for teaching me so much. I will always be grateful to her. I think what I missed more than anything, during all the war years, was being cuddled by my parents.

Documenting my evacuee memories prompted me to do some reading on the subject. I found it interesting to learn of the impact the Evacuation had on the social fabric of the country, which is not generally known. It hadn't been really recognised just how much poverty and deprivation existed in the country until the children, particularly those from the East End of London, mixed with the rest of the population for the first time ever. After the war, class distinction became less marked and politicians became determined to improve conditions for the poor, elderly and needy.

Consequently, there was a sharp increase in the building of council houses for the workers and nutritional programmes were set up, to inform and help mothers with the health of their children. A child allowance was given to mothers of newly born babies, to help with necessities. Also, there is an almost direct link with the Evacuation and the setting up of the National Health Service, which was intended to provide free treatment for those who needed it. The final result was a vast social improvement in Britain.

# POSTSCRIPT TO JUST JULIET

When I was due to give my first talk (I have since given many), I asked Bryan and Myriam if they had any memories to add to mine. Bryan had very few, but Myriam had more, mainly very unhappy ones. Most of Myriam's memories and the few that Bryan's sent me originally are incorporated in 'Just Juliet'. When I read the story to Myriam before it was printed, it made her cry. Three years ago I had a wonderful surprise and *I* almost cried with *joy*. Remember the bracelet that I gave Myriam as part of her birthday presents when I was about nine and later asked for it back? Well she said "Hold out your hand, I have something for you" and there nestling in my hand was the little gold bracelet, after all these years! It still fits too and I love it. Thankyou so much Myriam.

After I sent a copy of 'Just Juliet' to Bryan, it seemed to unleash endless memories, page after page, including memories of his earlier life in Harpenden, enough in fact to write his own book. I thought the rest of his evacuee memories ought to be included in this book.

# BRYANS MEMORIES AS TOLD TO JULIET

After we three children were forcibly split up on arrival in Derby, Bryan and his group were taken to the village hall in Hartshorne. Eventually a lady came to collect him. Her husband was a miner and they also had a lot of poultry houses, which meant that Bryan spent an interesting time collecting eggs and working with the chickens. They were a pleasant family and fed him well and her parents ran a sweet shop, an advantage in the days of rationing!

Bryan discovered that during wartime, if you relinquished your egg ration, you could opt for chicken feed instead and a similar scheme operated for pig food. If you exercised these options, you didn't necessarily consume all the eggs and bacon yourselves but could exchange them for other things which were in short supply, such as sugar etc.

Near Hartshorne was Swadlincote, a pottery producing area where local children used to search through the spoil tips looking for unglazed pottery, which they would paint and sell for pocket money. The evacuees from Chalkwell School Westcliff had lessons in an old Sunday-School building at the top of the village, and in the middle of the village was the local school. Bryan's billet was at the lower end, and he soon learned to make his way 'home' after school, across the fields to avoid the road where the local children would be waiting to harass him.

Bryan thinks it was ironic that we were evacuated to areas near Derby, which with Rolls Royce supplying most of the aircraft engines at that time, was an obvious target for the Germans. Bryan and the family frequently had to use the air raid shelters. Most of the bombs fell in fields, creating great interest for the boys, but on one occasion a bomb fell directly on the shop owned by the parents of Bryan's foster mother. The elderly couple, who had been sheltering under the stairs, were saved but the shock must have been too much as the old lady died soon after.

Having heard that he had passed the Grammar School scholarship exam that he had taken before we were evacuated, it was now time for Bryan to move to a new school. He said he remembers taking the scholarship for Westcliff High School, which as far as he knows, was evacuated to Belper, in Derbyshire. However, he is not quite sure how he ended up with the Southend Grammar School, which was evacuated to the Queen Elizabeth Grammar School for Boys, Mansfield. He thinks it must have been something to do with our father. Was it that he had heard that the standard was better, or did he want us to be nearer to him, who knows? All I do know is that going to Mansfield instead of staying in Derbyshire adversely affected we three children's lives.

Bryan found it very depressing and difficult, moving from a small village school in a rural area, to a large Grammar School in Mansfield, and felt very vulnerable for a long time. Frequently in trouble with the teaching staff, he became a regular visitor to the headmaster's study to be caned, but on a more positive note, was able to shine at German and Religious Education. Clearly his early upbringing had some benefit, and he had retained what Father had taught him.

Worse was to come though when he was 'abducted' by Father and taken to his lodgings at Ruddington near Nottingham, where Julius was working as a Checker at the sugar beet factory. As the new school term was due to start, Bryan was sent along to the local school on the first day, but as the other children, knowing each other already, gradually paired off, Bryan was left on his own, feeling very lonely and vulnerable yet again

When the 'abduction' came to an end after intervention by
Mother, Bryan was sent for safekeeping to The Seventh Day
Adventist Training College at Newbold Revel near Rugby in
Warwickshire, some 40 or 50 miles south of Mansfield. This
was chosen because Mother's brother and sister were students
there. The College was a self-sufficient commune, and
alongside receiving tuition in all subjects, especially religious
instruction, students were all expected to work, both on the
farm and in the College. One skill that Bryan acquired was as a
Silver Service Waiter!

*BRYAN IN HIS GRAMMAR SCHOOL UNIFORM*

Eventually this chapter came to an end when the Court granted
Mother custody of we three children. Bryan returned to Mansfield,

going to various billets. While in Mansfield, Bryan led quite a full life, joining the choir at the St John's Church, the Scouts, and later, the Army Cadet Corps, which came under the auspices of the St John's Church. He also joined the Air Training Corps through his school. He found the Cadet uniform had advantages for hitch hiking, which was a common and accepted means of transport in wartime. During the war and for many years after, drivers never ignored service personnel wanting a lift and in his Cadet uniform Bryan was often mistaken for a regular army soldier.

Bryan has memories of working hard and playing hard, including camping, in the Peak District with the Scouts and in the grounds of Chatsworth with the Army Cadets. During one stay in the Peak District, a Wellington bomber crashed in the hills, it was returning in a damaged condition from a raid on Germany. Although the rest of the crew were killed, the rear gun turret broke off and the rear gunner was thrown out. He managed to find his way in the pitch dark to a house, where he was helped. The scouts were forbidden to go near the wreck but most of them did, including Bryan and all took away a 'trophy'. His was the chevron from the plane's side, which he hid away wrapped in a blanket, that was returning by separate transport. He never saw the 'trophy' again!

One of Bryan's billets in Mansfield was with Mr & Mrs Sage, where he had a somewhat strained relationship with their son Barry. This was not a particularly happy billet for Bryan, who regularly ran away, usually to Gate Burton Hall in Lincolnshire where Mother was now working as a midwife. He would cycle there, and always made for the kitchen first where the cook, who had a soft spot for Bryan, would make sure he was well fed before informing Mother that once more, he had arrived. Bryan was made to feel very welcome by all the staff and given overnight accommodation.

Now came the time when I, Juliet, had to move from dear little Mrs Tallon's house because she was moving into an Old People's bungalow and couldn't take me with her. Bryan valiantly offered to move out so that I could move into the Sage's house, as I already knew them so well. However billets were hard to find and he was lodged temporarily in a Hostel for boys who were classed as not fitting easily into normal homes. In charge of the Hostel were a French lady and her daughter, it was very well managed and the boys were given excellent food. However every Friday at teatime, the boys were expected to eat a large raw onion and take a laxative tablet! The boys slept in dormitories and had their own leisure room where they organised many things as a group, writing their own newspaper etc. In spite of the Hostel being for 'bad' boys Bryan was very happy there and was sorry when the time came to leave

Bryan's last billet was with an elderly lady whose sister had a small confectionery shop, (in luck again) and for a while he was Assistant Cub Master for a troupe at Bull Farm Estate. The Cub Master was a Bevin Boy, so called after Ernest Bevin, the Minister for Labour in the Coalition Government. This was a scheme devised in a desperate attempt to raise the production of coal, whereby one in every ten men due to be called up for the forces was chosen, by ballot, to go down the mines instead. It was not very popular due to the lack of glamour associated with the forces and the hard work down the mines.

The total evacuation experience took a heavy toll on Bryan, and by the time we all moved to Sturton-by-Stow at the end of the war, he was completely run down, both mentally and physically. It was therefore decided that a spell of farm work would be beneficial even though the hours were long and the pay low. Later he was to join the Navy, perhaps influenced by his time in the ACC and the ATC at Mansfield.

# OVERSEAL

After I had given my first 'evacuee' talk, my husband Clive asked me if I would like to rediscover the places to which I had been evacuated. My stomach lurched and I felt quite ill. However, after some thought, I decided that I would quite like to go back to Overseal where I did have some happy times. Not to MANSFIELD though, the very name gives me the creeps!

So we took ourselves to Overseal near Burton-on-Trent, to try to locate the house where I had been so happy. I still have my 8th birthday card from my brother, a Mickey Mouse postcard with the address of the Eyre family on it as Burton Road, but no house number. I remembered that the house was at the edge of the village and had a fairly long driveway, but couldn't be sure which house it was. As there had been a son and a daughter, I wondered if any relatives would be still living in the village.

I spotted a postman on his round and thought that he would probably know everyone in the village. However, on asking if he knew of anyone named Eyre, he said he didn't but he had only been working there for a short time. However his mother in law had been the post-lady for some years and may have more information. When we located her she said she didn't recognise the name, but as she had only been doing the job for about 15 years suggested that maybe the previous post-lady, Cynthia would be able to help, as she had lived in the village all her life.

We were in luck as Cynthia was at home, and welcomed us in when we explained our mission. Amazingly Cynthia knew the Butlers, it seems that Cynthia's parents and the Butlers had been friends and somewhere she had a photo of them. She told us that both were now deceased and that the house where they had lived was just round the corner, so after we left, we went to see it and took a photograph. The house was just as I remembered, in the middle of a row of three and we could see the back garden where Myriam and I had played (except on Sundays!).

Cynthia also told us that she did know the Eyre family but couldn't remember where they had lived. However, she remembered Mrs Eyre's maiden name and told us that some of her relatives may live in another village not far away and gave us a rough idea of the address. Cynthia was so helpful, phoning various people while we were there. She even spoke to a friend who also had evacuees from Westcliff and gave me the names of the two girls but they didn't mean anything to me. Later we did try to find the relatives in the area that Cynthia suggested, but without success.

Cynthia told us that in the village was a man who ran a bicycle shop and she thought he might know where the Eyres had lived, as he had been in the village for very many years. So off we went (just like a detective story this) and found the shop, but the man said the name didn't sound familiar and he had only been there since 1951! However, he told us that just across the road was a lady of 90 named Alice and she had lived in the village all her life, "But it looks as if she is just going out, in a car". I dashed across the road to catch her and explained what I was after. Alice kindly gave us her phone number and asked us to return another time and to bring our lovely Old English Sheepdog Katie, who was in the car with us. Her brother had come to take her to a party, for her 91st birthday and she was going to her sister's house in MANSFIELD!

Having kept in touch with Cynthia and Alice, we later arranged a second visit to Overseal. By this time 'Just Juliet' had been printed so we went armed with several copies. We first went to see Cynthia who told us that she had left more information and photographs with Alice. She also told us that she had located the house where the Eyre family had lived and suggested that we go to the village Post Office to see Jenny, who worked there, as she would be able to help us more.

Jenny was expecting us, and was most helpful. It seems that she had lived all her life in the house next door to the Eyres. When she gave us the address we realised that we had been looking at the wrong end of the village (thanks to the wrong address on my brother's postcard) and it was not Burton Road after all. Jenny told us that she had left a photograph of the Eyre family with Alice. She knew them well of course, and told us that sadly, Frank (who teased me so much), had died suddenly of a heart attack about 10 years previously. He had been married with a son and a daughter. Dorothy had married a Polish soldier and they had a son, twin boys and a girl, but none of the Eyre family was now living in the village and Jenny had lost touch with them all.

At last we found the house and sure enough, it looked familiar and it was still, together with the semi next door (Jenny's house), the last house in the village. There was the country lane that I remembered walking down and running down as I 'left home' when Frank had teased me! So we decided we would like to take a photograph of the house, and since it was quite isolated, knocked on the door to seek permission, and were invited in by the new owner Cliff, for coffee and to have a chat. He told us that he and his wife (now deceased) had actually bought the house from Mr Eyre in 1958, sadly Mrs Eyre had died before then. Cliff was born in 1927 and Frank was about the same age, so they were contemporaries, although they hadn't attended the same school. Cliff went to the Church of England School (now demolished and replaced by the Community Centre) known as the Bottom School. That must have been the one that Myriam went to, and I must have been at the Top School. I had remembered correctly that there were two schools.

Cliff told us a strange tale. When he left school, for several years he worked for a local Baker and remembers delivering bread to the Eyre household. On one occasion he had a very strong feeling that, at some time in the future, he would live there. In 1958 he and his wife had been about to buy another house in the district but the sale fell through at the last minute. By a series of events they came to hear from their solicitor that the Eyre house was for sale, and they were able to purchase it. Cliff had made a few alterations and had built on an extension to the house but it did take me back and certainly the front drive looked the same. I had a lovely 'warm' feeling to be in that house again, after so many years. Cliff also knew the Butlers.

After lunch we kept our appointment with Alice, by then almost 92. What a delight that was, she was so enthusiastic and entertained us royally with tea and home made cakes. She played the piano with gusto and sang to us, which we recorded. She lived in a lovely old house with a fantastic garden all on her own. She told us how her family and friends always came to her house for parties (except on her birthdays) and these parties were quite frequent. She was so fit and active with a wonderfully fertile mind.

Alice was able to tell us lots of stories of Overseal in wartime and, thanks to Cynthia and Jenny, we had some photographs to look at. Also Cynthia had left a letter for us with more information. She had even been to see the relatives of the Eyres that she had told us about, but they had lost touch with the family. One photograph in particular was a real gem. It was of Dorothy Eyre's wedding and there, just as I remembered them were Mr and Mrs Eyre, Dorothy, her husband of course, Frank and his wife who was Matron of Honour and others including Jenny, who was a bridesmaid. Oh what joy, it was taken in front of the house as it *had* been in 1940, and it brought back so many memories. Jenny gave us permission to borrow the photograph to get it copied and it is something I will always treasure.

Alice was a native of Mansfield, and her father had been a winder in the Colliery. She had three sisters and they had all been educated at the Queen Elizabeth Grammar School, which Myriam and I had attended. She also knew our previous school, Carter Lane Mixed School Mansfield, very well. Alice told us that it was at the top of the hill going out of town, about 800yards from the Rock Houses, one of which was still occupied. Her younger sister was now in a Nursing Home very near to the school. Alice also said that the standard at Carter Lane School was very high. Now that made me feel much better. Looking at my aged 10 School Report from Carter Lane, (sent to me some years ago by Valerie Sage), I thought my marks were not too bad. However I was only placed 34th out of a class of 45 and that was with 593 marks out of a total of 800 possible. 'Ought to be better' was the remark by the class teacher. When Valerie sent it to me she obviously also thought it was not a very good performance and said I must have improved over the years to get where I was in my Nursing career!

Alice became very special to us and we kept in touch by letters and phone calls. We were due to visit her again but received a short note written by her in very shaky handwriting, to say she had been in hospital after becoming very distressed following a break-in at her house and would we delay our visit? The next time we heard was from a relative to say that dear courageous Alice had died. It seems she had suffered another break in, it had made her so ill she went into a Care Home and very soon after had died. We were so very sad and angry to think she had been hounded to her death and made to leave her beautiful old house, which she so loved; what a tragedy.

I will always be grateful to the wonderful people of Overseal, for their help and kindness in helping me find the house where Myriam and I had been so happy. If only we could have spent the rest of the war with the caring Eyre family in the lovely rural village of Overseal, Myriam and I would have had a very different tale to tell. Bryan too, if only he could have remained in Hartshorne.

# JULIUS

I learned that my father Julius did various jobs during the war. He moved to the Midlands just before we were evacuated, and it must have been hard for him, after having his own business. He did try working as a bus conductor for a while, but had to keep stopping the bus to be sick! Needless to say that job didn't last long. Then he worked as a Checker in a sugar beet factory, and there were several other jobs but I have no details of them. Finally he started his own business, in Industrial Cleaning with a cleaning powder called Ensign Nordust. I still have some of his advertising pencils, which he obviously gave away to customers. The pencils are 3 faceted and on each side is written an eye-catching motto as follows:

1)   Neither Dirt NORDUST Cleaners Trust.

2)   Dust Absorbing ENSIGN NORDUST Disinfecting.

3)   Tested As Best ENSIGN NORDUST Sweeping Success.

At the top of the pencil is his Beeston phone number. I understand that the business was quite successful even though it was a one-man band, well almost. He had contracts with schools and factories, to supply them with the powder and he employed an elderly gentleman to mix the 'ingredients' which was done in his garage. He once told me they only consisted of sawdust and disinfectant powder! Very effective though.

Julius was a great one for gimmicky words. He once told me that my name, Juliet was made from our parent's names, Julius and Violet! Our house in Harpenden was called NORDHEIM (part of his surname Norden and 'heim' means 'home' in German) and the bungalow in Westcliff was called BRYMYJU (from BRYan, MYriam and JUliet).

I think my father must have had a lot of sadness in his life. Our parents never lived together again after the war, but were never divorced. I don't think he ever stopped loving my mother and never gave up hope of reconciliation.

*JULIUS*

Many of his friends and relatives perished in the holocaust. His youngest sister Rosa (my aunt), her husband Jacob Rosemann, and their youngest daughter Irmgard, all died in Sobibor Concentration Camp in 1943, whilst their eldest daughter Martha died in Auschwitz in 1944. My father's cousin Ernst Kaufmann also died in Auschwitz in1944 and his wife Kaete (nee Norden and a distant relative) perished in Theresienstadt Concentration Camp in 1943.

Julius died in 1964, aged 80.

# HAMBURG

In recent times we have discovered where my father was actually born in Hamburg. Our son Kevin found the street and the site of the building, (with the same address) which was almost certainly demolished when Britain bombed Hamburg at the end of July 1943.

60% of all homes in the city were destroyed in these raids, killing more than 40,000 citizens, with nearly as many again injured. A modern office block now occupies the site and in the entrance foyer is a painting of the street as it was in the 19th century. In the painting, a coach and horses are seen coming out of an archway, which may be where the entrance to the offices now is. At the top of the hill, on the painting, is a lovely little church, which is still there. Inside the church Kevin found another similar painting of the street showing the old houses before it was redeveloped. He said that he had a very strange feeling to be in the area, in the very same street, where his grandfather was born.

I wrote the following poem when writing 'Just Juliet', to sum up my whole experience.

The Enemy is coming
It's time to start running
Time to EVACUATE

Grab hold of your Gasmasks
Just think of those tasks
Were we told to EVACUATE

Here is my knapsack
Oh please put that back
I must take my favourite Teddy

In goes my new book
A toy, sandwiches, fruit
Undies, socks, sponge bag, I'm ready

A label is tied to my coat
I have such a lump in my throat
As we troop off to our school

We bus to the station
Where everyone's waiting
Don't cry, I'll feel such a fool

Now onto the steam train
It's no longer a game
As we're packed in like little sardines

The journey is endless
I'm frightened and friendless
We've arrived, have I got everything

To the village hall we go
And how was I to know
Many people didn't really want us

We're all lined up like cattle
Gone now is my prattle
Please some-one won't you choose us

At last we're taken 'home'
As well it wasn't known
This was only the first of ten billets

I was seven when I went
I knew we had to be sent
But oh this war we must win it

After five long years away
I'll never forget the day
When at last I'm home to stay

HIP HIP HOORAY!

My mother died in September 2000, aged 94. She always felt a bit guilty for sending us away and yet what else could she have done? At least she kept an eye on us, and soon had us moved to a new billet when things were unsatisfactory. Having read in recent times how badly some evacuees were treated by their foster parents, I think on the whole we got off lightly. However there is no doubt that we were all quite traumatised by the whole episode and that it has had a profound effect on all our lives.

# MANSFIELD EDUCATION COMMITTEE.

## CARTER LANE MIXED SCHOOL.

TERM REPORT *Dec 1942*     Name *Juliet Norden*

Form *IV N*     Number in Class *45*     Position in Class *34*

| Subject | Marks Possible | Marks Obtained | Remarks |
|---|---|---|---|
| Reading | 100 | 79 | *g+* |
| Composition | 100 | 75 | *g* |
| English | 100 | 87 | *g+* |
| Arithmetic | 100 | 76 | *g+* |
| History | 100 | 86 | *g+* |
| Science | 100 | 64 | *fair* |
| Geography | 100 | 56 | *weak* |
| Mental Art | 100 | 70 | *g.* |
| Needlework | | | |
| **TOTAL** | **800** | **593** | *Ought to be better* |

Conduct *g.*

General Remarks *This girl does not concentrate. She is too sure & consequently her whole mind is not on the work in hand*

Class Teacher *Worsey*

Head Teacher *A.H. Naylor*

1.250/1241